# CONTENTS

# SPIES AND SPYING

The world of the secret agent can seem glamorous – parachuting behind enemy lines or grabbing secrets. In reality, however, spying is a tough business. Spies trust no-one and could be revealed at any time.

## WHY DO IT?

People become spies for many reasons. Some betray their country for cash. Others are blackmailed into handing over secrets. A few spy just for excitement. Of course, they all need to be able to keep a secret!

In movies, spies get into fights all the time. In real life, agents avoid attention. They try not to use secret gadgets and weapons. Charm is a more useful tool for getting information out of people!

## VARIED SKILLS

Spies need to be patient. It can take many years in a job before they get their hands on important documents. They also need guts. Spies who get caught are often tortured by their enemies. Today's spies are trained to resist torture. Recruits are deprived of food, water and sleep, and are often bombarded with questions.

THERE IS

ALBERT R. BROCCOLI PRESENTS PIERCE BROSNAN AS JAMES BOND 007 IN 'GOLD
DIRECTOR OF PHOTOGRAPHY PHIL MEHEUX PRODUCTION DESIGNER PETER LAMONT EXECUTIVE PRODUCER TO

CH

# SPIES

## Behind Enemy Lines

WAYLAND

First published in 2011 by Wayland

Copyright © 2011 Brown Bear Books Ltd.

Wayland
Hachette Children's Books
338 Euston Road
London NW1 3BH

Wayland Australia
Level 17/207 Kent Street
Sydney, NSW 2000

Brown Bear Books Ltd.
First Floor
9–17 St. Albans Place
London
N1 0NX

**Editor:** Tim Cooke
**Designer:** Joanne Mitchell
**Picture researcher:** Clare Newman
**Art director:** Jeni Child
**Editorial director:** Lindsey Lowe
**Production director:** Alastair Gourlay
**Children's publisher:** Anne O'Daly

British Library Cataloguing in Publication Data
Spies : behind enemy lines. -- (Mission
    impossible)
    1. Espionage--Pictorial works--Juvenile
    literature.
    I. Series
    327.1'2-dc22

ISBN: 978 0 7502 6545 4

Printed in China
Wayland is a division of Hachette Children's Books,
an Hachette UK company.
www.hachette.co.uk

**Websites**
The website addresses (URLs) included in this
book were valid at the time of going to press.
However, because of the nature of the internet, it is
possible that some addresses may have changed,
or sites may have changed or closed down sibnce
publication. While the author and publisher regret
any inconvenience this may cause the readers, no
responsibility for any such changes can be accepted
by either the author or the publisher.

## PICTURE ACKNOWLEDGEMENTS

**Front Cover: Shutterstock**

**Interior: Corbis:** Bettmann 11tr, 14br, 17tr, Richard
A. Bloom 12cl, Ramon Marient 7t; **iStockphoto:**
Alengo 5cr, Eduardo Antonio Fuentes 8/9, Manuel
Gutjahr 3, Jim Lopez 5tr, Pali Rao 5br, Mark
Wragg 31; **Photolibrary:** Japanese Travel Bureau
8bl; **Robert Hunt Library:** 10/11, 12cl, 12/13, 18/19;
**Shutterstock:** Andrey Burmakin 23tr, C&O Photo
28tr, Elnur 21t, Mark R. Higgins 24tc, Mihalec 9tr,
Raedwald 16/17, Scouting Stock 14/15; **The Kobal
Collection:** Danjaq/EON/UE 4/5, EON/Danjaq/
Sony 28/29; **Thinkstock:** 20/21, 22/23, 24/25, 27t;
**Topham:** 13tl, 15br, 16tc, 18bl, 19br, 28cl, AP 26bc,
EPA 20bl, Keystone Archive/HIP 26/27, Public
Record Office/HIP 25bl, The Granger Collection 6tc,
10cl, The Print Collector/HIP 6/7.

◁ *James Bond is one idea of a spy – but the reality is less glamorous and dramatic.*

ITUTE

DON BAKER ASSOCIATE PRODUCERS ANTHONY WAYE EDITOR TERRY RAWLINGS
MICHAEL G. WILSON AND BARBARA BROCCOLI DIRECTED BY MARTIN CAMPBELL

△ **Top**: *A spy uses a telephoto lens for secret surveillance.* **Middle**: *False fingerprints help agents get through identity checks.* **Bottom**: *Computers are full of secrets – if you know how to hack into them.*

# A MASTER OF DISGUISE

In the 1750s, King Louis of France sent Chevalier d'Eon on a secret mission to Russia. He decided it would be best if he disguised himself as a woman, Lia de Beaumont. For almost 50 years, d'Eon kept people guessing about his identity.

## THE PERFECT SPY

Born in 1728, d'Eon grew up with a gift for languages, a remarkable memory – and a skill for fencing. He came to the notice of the French king, Louis XV, when he attended a fancy-dress ball dressed as a woman. The king thought that a woman would make a perfect spy. D'Eon looked the part, with narrow shoulders and a small build.

## GOING UNDERCOVER

Louis sent d'Eon to the court of Empress Elizabeth of Russia. Relations between the two countries were tense. D'Eon met the empress in private and handed over a letter from Louis containing a secret agreement. As a result, friendly relations between France and Russia were soon restored.

△ *D'Eon fenced against the Prince of Wales while wearing women's clothes.*

◁ *People were fascinated by the idea of men dressing as women. D'Eon became a celebrity.*

### MAN OR WOMAN?

In 1762, Louis sent d'Eon to London. The king wanted to make an alliance with England (but also to see if it was possible for the French to invade). But then d'Eon disobeyed an order to return home. He began to claim that he really was a woman, hoping that would protect him from being killed by the king's agents. Soon the whole of London was guessing whether he was a man or a woman. The truth only came out when he died in 1810, at the age of 81!

## TOP SECRET

Spies disguise themselves in many ways. Padding changes your body shape. Stooping makes you look older. Props such as hats, scarves and glasses can be used to cover up. In the 1960s and 1970s, Antonio Mendez, chief of disguise for the CIA, used rubber cement, scissors and make-up to transform U.S. secret agents.

# SHADOW WARRIORS

In 1578, the Japanese warlord Uesugi Kenshin was murdered in his own lavatory. The assassin had crept into the castle unseen. He then hid for days in the pit below the toilet. When the time came, he struck with his short spear. Who was this deadly warrior lurking in the shadows?

△ *Uesugi Kenshin had no defence against the killer in his lavatory.*

## ASSASSINS FOR HIRE

In 15th-century Japan, warriors acted as spies and assassins for the rival warlords who battled to control the country. These warriors were called ninjas.

In Japanese *ninja* means 'someone who moves stealthily'. The ninjas were trained in close combat, disguise, silent entry and escape. They could swim in full armour and climb tall castle walls using hooked ropes. They used weapons such as throwing stars, claws, daggers and swords. Their exploits made them legendary. But the ninja were not always noble heroes. Some were cold-blooded and ruthless killers.

▷ *The ninja were famous for the ultra-sharp blades of their swords.*

## NIGHT RAID

Night attacks were a favourite ninja tactic. One story from the 1300s tells how a 13-year-old named Kumawaka set out to avenge the death of his father, Lord Suketomo.

The young man crept towards the room of Hommo Saburo, the monk who had ordered his father's death. A lamp burnt brightly in the room, so the teenager opened the door. This allowed moths to swarm in and put out the light.

Kumawaka grabbed Saburo's sword. Waking the monk, he then plunged the blade into Saburo's body. Kumawaka fled, chased by guards who had heard their master's cries. Faced with a deep moat, he climbed up a thick bamboo shoot. Kumawaka used his weight to bend the tip down to drop over on the other side of the moat and escape.

# TOP SECRET

Like ninjas, spies throughout the ages have learnt to make themselves 'invisible'. In a crowd, they try to blend in. They walk silently and smoothly, using cover such as trees and walls. At night, they stay in the shadows and keep away from lit windows.

# CIVIL WAR CHARMERS

During the American Civil War (1861–1865) some of the most effective spies were women. They found it easy to learn secrets and to pass them to the enemy.

◁ Belle Boyd visits Confederate prisoners in a Union army stockade at Manassas Junction, Virginia.

## DODGING BULLETS

Belle Boyd learned secrets by flirting with Union officers staying at her father's hotel. She used false papers to smuggle her secrets through Union lines to the Confederates. Belle was famous for being a fast talker. Everyone knew she was a spy. In just four years, she was arrested six times and put in prison twice. But Belle always charmed her way out.

## THE WILD ROSE

Beautiful Southerner Rose O'Neal Greenhow was invited to all the best parties in Washington, D.C. Like Belle, she supported the Confederacy. And like Belle, she charmed Union officers and politicians into revealing important secrets. But in 1861, Union spymaster Allan Pinkerton's agents investigated her. They found military maps in her home. Greenhow was put in prison. But even behind bars, the 'Wild Rose' continued to gather and pass on information.

▽ *Rose O'Neal Greenhow and her daughter in prison.*

## TOP SECRET

Civil war spies found new ways to pass on information. Belle Boyd hid notes inside a hollow watch. Rose O'Neal Greenhow sent signals by the position of the blinds and candles in her prison window. She even hid a message inside a visitor's hair bun. Confederate spies also photographed and shrank messages so they could be hidden inside metal buttons.

11

1011101001010100100010101101001101001

# CAN YOU KEEP A SECRET?

On D-Day, 1944, 160,000 Allied troops landed on the beaches of Normandy in northern France. The next day, British spy Violette Szabo landed in France. Her mission: to disrupt German forces heading to fight the invaders.

## SABOTEUR!

Four years earlier, Violette had met and married a French soldier in London. After he was killed fighting the Germans in 1942, she decided to become a spy. She was trained in navigation, escape, weapons and explosives, unarmed combat and using radios and codes. At first, her officers doubted whether she was up to the job.

▷ *Coded messages were broadcast from Britain to the French Resistance: owning an illegal radio in France could lead to imprisonment or death.*

△ *The British trained Violette Szabo to help local fighters to sabotage German forces.*

### SAY NOTHING!

Violette's first mission was a success. Code-named 'Louise', she was dropped into France to become a saboteur. She helped a group of local fighters blow up roads and railway bridges to stop the Germans moving around.

A month later, Violette was back in France for D-Day. Within days, her team was ambushed by a German patrol. Violette was injured during the gun battle. The others escaped, but she kept firing until she ran out of bullets and was captured. Violette was then tortured by the Gestapo for several weeks, but never told her torturers anything.

Violette was finally sent to Germany and put in a concentration camp, where she was starved and forced to do hard labour. She was executed on 5 February, 1945, aged just 23.

## TOP SECRET

Every spy feared being captured by the Gestapo, the German secret police. They tortured prisoners in terrible ways: removing fingernails, giving them electric shocks or half-drowning them in bathtubs. The British trained agents to make up a cover story rather than reveal the truth. Spies still had to be incredibly brave and determined to survive the pain of torture.

# SPIES IN THE SKY

During the Cold War of the 1950s and 1960s, the U.S. government worried that the Soviet Union might bomb America. To find out more, they developed a new spy plane to photograph Soviet air bases. It was called the U-2.

## ENGINE TROUBLE

The plane was designed so that it could fly too high to be hit by Soviet missiles. But in May 1960, engine trouble forced U.S. pilot Gary Powers to fly lower than usual. A Soviet missile exploded close to his U-2, throwing him from the aircraft before he could make it self-destruct. He parachuted to the ground, but was captured. The U-2 crashed – but its equipment was not damaged. The Soviets were able to learn all the spy plane's secrets.

▽ An American spy plane took this photo of a site in Cuba in 1962, showing that the Soviets had set up a missile base there.

MISSILE ERECTOR

CABLE

MISSILE SHELTER TENT

TRACKED PRIME MOVERS

FUEL TANK TRAILERS

OXIDIZER TANK TRAILERS

# TOP SECRET

The cameras inside the U-2 could 'see' objects on the ground as small as 30 centimetres (12 inches) across. They could also take over 4,000 pictures in a single mission. Modern spy planes like the A-12 (left) are also fitted with antennas to pick up radio signals, emails and telephone calls.

## LOST IN ACTION?

After the crash, the U.S. government assumed that the aircraft had been destroyed and that Powers had been killed. They said the aircraft had been lost on a mission to study the weather.

The Americans were very embarrassed when the Soviet leader Nikita Khrushchev announced that Powers was alive. At a televised trial, the pilot confessed he was a spy. The wreck of the plane was also put on display. Powers was found guilty of spying and sentenced to 10 years in jail.

In fact, Powers came home far sooner. In 1962, he returned to the United States after being swapped for a Soviet spy caught in Germany.

△ Gary Powers holds a model of the U-2 at his televised trial in Moscow.

# SPY NETWORK

During the 1930s, the Soviet secret service recruited five former students from Britain's elite Cambridge University. They were communists who supported the Soviet government. After university, they became 'moles', getting jobs that allowed them to pass on secrets.

## UNDERCOVER MOLES

One of the five, Anthony Blunt, worked for British military intelligence in World War II. He passed on details about eastern European governments that helped the Soviets take over their countries after the war. Another mole, John Cairncross, helped crack German codes during the war. He passed over 5,800 messages straight to the Russians.

△ (Clockwise from top right) Blunt, Philby, Maclean and Burgess were all members of the 'Establishment'.

## ARCH TRAITOR

A third spy, Kim Philby, revealed the identities of U.S. and British agents to the Soviets. Most were tortured and executed. He also passed on U.S. nuclear secrets.

## ESCAPE TO RUSSIA

The last two members of the ring, Donald Maclean and Guy Burgess, also passed nuclear secrets to the Russians, and Maclean warned the Soviets that the Americans had cracked their 'Venona' code.

The Americans tracked the leak to an agent code-named 'Homer'. They sent Philby to investigate, but he had already warned 'Homer' – who was his friend Maclean.

In 1951, Maclean and Burgess escaped to Russia. Philby was sacked from his job and finally moved to Russia himself in 1963.

△ *Ethel and Julius Rosenberg leave court during their trial; they were executed in 1953 for passing secrets to the Russians.*

# TOP SECRET

U.S. codebreaker Meredith Knox Gardner decoded secret telegrams sent from New York to Moscow from 1943 to 1945. His remarkable breakthrough revealed dozens of Soviet spies working across the United States. Among them were husband and wife Julius and Ethel Rosenberg. They were arrested and executed for passing on nuclear secrets to the Russians.

# DUTCH DANCER

M ata Hari was the most famous spy of World War I (1914–1918). The Dutch dancer's real name was Margaretha Zelle: she was famous for her affairs with generals and politicians. When war broke out, a German official persuaded her to become a spy.

## A DOUBLE AGENT

The Netherlands was neutral, so Mata Hari was free to travel all over Europe. The French and British kept track of her because she knew so many senior officers on all sides. When Mata Hari offered to spy for the French, they agreed. She was dating a German official, so they hoped she could pass on secrets. In fact, Mata Hari was acting as a double agent. She was also too interested in enjoying herself to be a good spy.

◁ *Mata Hari used special ink to send secret messages to her German spymaster.*

## CAUGHT!

In January 1917, French agents intercepted a telegram from Madrid about 'agent H-21'. They identified H-21 as Mata Hari. She was arrested and accused of spying.

Mata Hari was found guilty (some modern experts think she was innocent). On 15 October, 1917, the dancer was executed by firing squad.

## TOP SECRET

Throughout history, spies have charmed secrets out of their lovers. King Charles II's lover Louise de Querouaille worked for the French king Louis XIV, for example. During the 1960s, the Soviet spy agency, the KGB, trained men and women to seduce Western diplomats. They were known as 'swallows' and 'ravens'. The meetings were photographed, then the spies blackmailed their victims into handing over secrets.

▽ *The Allies parade through Paris after the end of the war in 1918.*

# THE POISON UMBRELLA

Georgi Markov was a famous writer who left Bulgaria in 1969. He moved to London, where he spoke out against the communist leaders of Bulgaria on the radio. They ordered the Bulgarian secret service to kill him – with a little help from the Russian KGB.

▽ *Georgi Markov was a leading critic of the communist government of Bulgaria.*

## FIRST AND SECOND ATTEMPTS

In 1978, Markov flew to Munich, Germany, to visit a radio station. A party was held in his honour. A Bulgarian agent was supposed to put a poison pill in his drink. The plan failed, but the Bulgarians didn't give up. Soon after, Markov was on holiday on the island of Sardinia. The assassins planned to leave poison on his car door handle or the walls of his room. But they didn't want to kill his wife or daughter, so again they waited.

▷ *The umbrella carried a tiny pellet containing the poison ricin.*

# TOP SECRET

Spy agencies have invented a host of deadly gadgets. In the 1960s, the KGB came up with a wallet that fired poison gas and tiny pistols hidden in cigarette packets. At the same time, U.S. agents plotted to kill Fidel Castro, the leader of Cuba. They hoped to infect his cigars with bacteria or pack them with explosives. They even planned to put a chemical in his boots to make his beard fall out!

## THIRD TIME LUCKY

Finally the KGB came up with a new weapon, which they passed to their Bulgarian allies. It was an umbrella that injected a tiny poison pellet into the victim from its tip.

In September 1978, Markov was waiting at a bus stop on London Bridge went he felt a sting in the back of his thigh. He looked around and saw a man picking up an umbrella from the ground. When Markov arrived at work, he noticed a small red pimple on his leg. Within a few hours, he developed a fever and was taken to hospital. Three days later, he was dead. The tiny poison pellet was found inside his leg. His attacker, Francesco Gullino, code named 'Piccadilly', has never been arrested.

# BUGGED!

In 1962, Aldrich Ames joined the CIA, the U.S. spy agency. He wanted to be an international agent. By 1985, he was fed up with his job and deep in debt. So Ames decided to swap secrets for cash. Soon he was a double agent – and $50,000 richer.

## A DEADLY TRADE

At first, Ames just wanted to pay off his debts. But he got greedy. He handed the Soviets a bag filled with secret documents. Soon Ames was betraying every secret he could. He revealed the names of every U.S. spy in the Soviet Union, leading to the deaths of at least 10 agents. In return, the KGB paid him $2.7 million.

◁ *In handcuffs and chains, Aldrich Ames leaves his trial in 1994.*

▷ *Modern bugs are so small that they can be hidden virtually anywhere and detected only by sophisticated equipment.*

## BIG SPENDER

The CIA knew there was a big problem. Twenty agents had vanished into thin air. At first, no one suspected Ames, even though he had bought a new house and a flashy sports car. But the net was closing in. Investigators started going through Ames' finances. It was soon clear he was spending a lot more than he was earning.

## SPYCATCHER

The FBI put bugs all over Ames' house. A bug in his computer recorded everything he typed on the keyboard. Finally, the FBI swooped. Agents arrested Ames in 1994. They were just in time. He was planning to escape to Russia the next day. Ames was tried and sentenced to life in prison.

## TOP SECRET

Bugs are tiny microphones that can be hidden in pens, walls, floors, lamps or furniture. Most give off radio signals that are picked up by receivers nearby. Some bugs only switch on when someone comes into the room. 'Gun' microphones can pick up conversations from across the street. Mobile phones can also be turned into microphones, even when they are switched off.

# CODEBREAKERS

During World War II, all sides sent important messages in secret codes or ciphers. The Germans used the Enigma machine, which looked like a typewriter but was far more complex. The Germans believed their codes were unbreakable.

▷ *The Enigma machine used a series of wheels and different settings to generate highly complex codes.*

## TOP SECRET

Britain's codebreakers were based at the top-secret Bletchley Park, or 'Station X'. Each group was known only by its hut number. The head of hut 8, Alan Turing, designed an early computer, called a bombe. This was hooked up to the Enigma machine to speed up the codebreaking. The bombes were so secret they were all destroyed at the end of the war.

## TOUGH ODDS

Enigma used different settings each day. The odds of breaking the codes were 150 million million million to one! But the Poles had an Enigma machine. Just before the war began in 1939, they told the British how it worked using a system of rotors. The British put together a team to try to crack the code. The key step was to get hold of the code books that told the Enigma operators what settings to use for the rotors each day.

## BOLD PLAN

Commander Ian Fleming, who later wrote the James Bond novels, came up with a dramatic plan. His idea was to crash a captured German plane into the sea at night, then ambush the ship that came to the rescue – and steal its code settings.

## ULTRA SECRET

Fleming's plan was never carried out. But a breakthrough came in June 1941. Several Enigma machines were captured, along with code books. That was all the codebreakers needed.

Soon the British and Americans were reading thousands of German messages. This intelligence was called 'Ultra'. It led to many successful attacks on German ships and submarines. It also stopped the Germans from being able to capture North Africa, shortening the war by up to two years.

▷ *Technicians at Bletchley Park used Colossus, the first electronic digital computer, to decipher German codes.*

# AGENT ZIGZAG

One December night in 1942, during World War II, a German spy parachuted into a Cambridgeshire field. His mission was to blow up a British aircraft factory. Instead, he went straight to the nearest farm, called the police and surrendered. Why?

### A NAZI SPY?

Eddie Chapman had joined the British army 10 years earlier. When he left, he turned to crime. Chapman blew up bank vaults with explosives. After being wanted by the police in Scotland, Chapman fled to the island of Jersey. But he was soon captured and sent to prison on the island. While Chapman was still behind bars, the Germans invaded. Chapman offered to work for them. The Germans trained him as a spy, code-named 'Fritz'. They believed he hated the British government for locking him up.

▽ *Eddie Chapman – photographed after the war – spent 10 years in jail for safebreaking before he became a spy.*

### I'LL KILL HITLER

When he parachuted into Britain in 1942, Chapman was interviewed by the secret service, MI5. Chapman offered to become a double agent; he even offered to blow up Hitler! MI5 code-named him 'Zigzag' and faked his attack on the Cambridgeshire aircraft factory, so the Germans would think he had completed his mission.

On his next mission, Chapman lied to the Germans that their V-1 rockets were hitting London. In fact, most were off-target.

### DOUBLE DARE

When the war ended, Chapman had survived his dangerous game. The British paid him a reward and pardoned his crimes. He had already been awarded a medal for bravery and given a yacht by the Germans!

△ Hitler (centre) was one of Chapman's suggested targets.

# TOP SECRET

Most of the German spies who landed in Britain were turned into double agents. They were used to pass on false information to the Germans. This was known as the double cross or XX system. One agent, code name Garbo, was based in Portugal. He helped to confuse the Germans over the D-Day landings. Another spy, known as Tricycle, tried unsuccessfully to warn the Americans about the Japanese attack on Pearl Harbor.

# THE ACE OF SPIES

To some, Sidney Reilly was one of the greatest secret agents. To others, he was just a clever con man. No one knew where he came from, where he went, or who he really was!

△ *Reilly planned to kidnap Lenin, founder of the Soviet Union.*

## IN DISGUISE

Reilly was born in Russia but moved to England in the 1890s. Acting as a police informer, he met William Melville, later head of the British secret service. In 1904, Melville asked Reilly to win over William D'Arcy, who owned oil rights in the Middle East. Reilly disguised himself as a priest, boarded D'Arcy's yacht and soon convinced D'Arcy that he should work with the British.

## TOP SECRET

The writer Ian Fleming said that he based superspy James Bond (right) on Sidney Reilly. Reilly certainly was a master of disguise. He was a crack shot and had a gift for languages. Like Bond, Reilly was a playboy who liked to drink and gamble. He was charming and had many love affairs. But he was also ruthless and elusive.

◁ Another of Reilly's kidnap targets was Leon Trotsky, who led the Red Army. The plan came to nothing.

## STEALING SECRETS

When World War I started in 1914, Reilly got a job in Germany at an arms factory. One night he broke into the offices to look at plans of the latest weapons being developed. When he was discovered, Reilly strangled the guard and then escaped to Russia.

## KIDNAP!

Reilly claimed he spent three weeks behind enemy lines in 1917. In reality, he spent most of the war in the United States selling arms. But in 1918 Reilly did come up with a daring plan to kidnap the Soviet leaders Lenin and Trotsky. The plot failed, and Reilly was forced to flee to London in disguise. He returned to Russia twice more, and was probably shot by Soviet agents in 1925. The legendary spy was dead. Or was he?

# GLOSSARY

**ambush** to wait in hiding then make a sudden attack.

**assassin** a murderer who kills to order because of the victim's beliefs, ideas or position; assassins often work for money.

**blackmail** threatening to reveal information about a person in order to force them to do something.

**bug** a small hidden microphone, for listening secretly.

**camouflage** a disguise that allows a person or thing to blend into the background.

**cipher** a code that substitutes individual letters or numbers for other letters or numbers.

**code** a system of substituting letters, numbers or words, or of using secret signs and symbols, in order to hide the content of a message.

**codebreaker** someone who works out how to read a secret code.

**code name** a secret name used in messages so that a spy's real identity is kept hidden.

**communist** – a supporter of the Soviet Union and other

countries where politics are based on the idea of centralised state control.

**contact** the person with whom a secret agent swaps information.

**Confederate** a supporter of the southern states in the American Civil War (1861–1865).

**disguise** clothing and make-up that is used to help an agent look like someone else.

**double agent** a spy who pretends to work for one side, when they are really working for their opponents.

**espionage** another word for spying.

**hard labour** being forced to work in prison, doing tough jobs like breaking up rocks.

**intelligence** secret information about an enemy or rival.

**kidnap** capturing and imprisoning a person against his or her will.

**moat** a deep ditch filled with water dug around a castle.

**mole** an agent who is secretly working for the enemy.

**navigation** the process of finding a way from one place to another.

**ninja** secret agents in medieval Japan trained in the martial arts.

**pardon** to let someone escape punishment for a crime.

**rendezvous** a meeting between two spies.

**saboteur** a secret agent who goes behind enemy lines in order to destroy railway lines, bridges and other valuable infrastructure.

**secret service** a government organisation responsible for controlling spies and watching out for enemy spies.

**spymaster** the leader of a spy ring or secret service.

**telegram** a message sent along wires or cables using code.

**unarmed combat** fighting with just your bare hands.

**Union** the northern states in the American Civil War (1861–1865).

**vault** a secure room, often in a bank, where money, valuables and documents are stored.

# FURTHER READING

## BOOKS

Brenna, Herbie. *The Spy's Handbook.* Faber and Faber, 2003.

Coleman, Janet Wyman. *Secrets, Lies, Gizmos and Spies: A History of Spies and Espionage.* Harry N. Abrams, Inc. 2006.

Crowdy, Terry. *The Enemy Within: A History of Spies, Spymasters and Espionage.* Osprey Publishing, 2009.

Deary, Terry. *Spies* (Horrible Histories Handbooks. Scholastic, 2009)

Dowswell, Paul, and Fergus Fleming. *Spies* (Usborne True Stories), Usborne, 2007.

Farman, John. *The Short and Bloody History of Spies.* San Val, 2002.

Fridell, Ron. *Spy Technology* (Cool Science). Lerner Publications, 2007.

Gifford, Clive. *Spies* (Kingfisher Knowledge). Kingfisher, 2004.

Gifford, Clive. *Spies and Spying.* Oxford University Press, 2010.

Langley, Andrew. *Codes and Codebreaking* (Spies and Spying). Franklin Watts, 2009.

Martin, Michael. *Spy Gear.* Edge Books, 2008.

O'Shei, Tim. *World War II Spies.* Edge Books, 2008.

O'Shei, Tim. *Cold War Spies.* Edge Books, 2008.

Owen, David. *Hidden Secrets.* Firefly Books Ltd, 2002).

Rauf, Don. *Killer Lipstick and Other Spy Gadgets* (24/7: Spy Files). Children's Press, 2007.

Scott, Corey. *Spies and Code Breakers: A Primary Source History* (In Their Own Words). Gareth Stevens Publishing, 2009.

Sweetman, Bill. *High-Altitude Spy Planes: The U-2s* (War Planes). Capstone Press, 2008.

Volkman, Ernest. *The History of Espionage.* Carlton Books, 2007.

Wagner, Heather Lehr, and Tim McNeese. *Spies in the Civil War* (Civil War: A Nation Divided). Chelsea House, 2009.

## WEBSITES

**http://www.spymuseum.org**
*Web site of the International Spy Museum in Washington, DC.*

**http://www.pbs.org/wgbh/nova/venona**
*PBS website with biographies of the atomic spies of the 1940s.*

**http://www.fbi.gov/aboutus.htm**
*Learn about past missions of the Federal Bureau of Investigation.*

**http://www.spyschool.com/spybios/sbmenu.htm**
*Profiles of the most famous and infamous spies.*

**http://www.mi5.gov.uk/output/history.html**
*Details of the past activies of MI5, Britain's secret service.*

**http://www.bletchleypark.org,uk**
*Website of the home of Britain's WWII codebreakers.*

# INDEX